# Living with an Addict

## Understanding the Hell of Addiction - Alcohol & Drug Abuse

By

**Biella Blom**

Living with an Addict: Understanding the Hell of Addiction - Alcohol & Drug Abuse

**Copyright © 2017**

All rights reserved. This book or any portion thereof may not be reproduced or used in any manner whatsoever without the express written permission of the publisher except for the use of brief quotations in a book review.

ISBN: 9781973200208

**Warning and Disclaimer**

Every effort has been made to make this book as accurate as possible. However, no warranty or fitness is implied. The information provided is on an "as-is" basis. The author and the publisher shall have no liability or responsibility to any person or entity with respect to any loss or damages that arise from the information in this book.

**Publisher Contact**

Skinny Bottle Publishing

books@skinnybottle.com

| | |
|---|---|
| Introduction | 1 |
| Dedication | 6 |
| **Chapter 1** | **7** |
| Understanding Addiction | 7 |
|     Defining a Drug Addict and an Alcoholic | 8 |
|     What Causes Addiction? | 10 |
| **Chapter 2** | **13** |
| Identifying Addiction | 13 |
|     What you Need to Know about Addict Behaviour | 14 |
|     Further Identifying a Loved One as an Addict | 16 |
|     How to Approach the Subject of Addiction | 18 |
| **Chapter 3** | **21** |
| Treatment and Finding Sobriety | 21 |
|     Planned Interventions | 21 |
|     Gradual Grooming | 23 |
|     Rehabilitation Centres and Half-Way Houses | 25 |
|     Long- Term Recovery | 27 |
| **Chapter 4** | **29** |
| Enabling and Co-Dependency | 29 |
|     Enabling | 29 |
|     Co-Dependency | 32 |

## Chapter 5 .................................................................................................................35

### What if the Addict is a Minor? ..............................................................35

#### Parents can Play a Role in Influencing their Child's Choices ................39

## Chapter 6 .................................................................................................................45

### Understanding the 3 C's ........................................................................45

## Chapter 7 .................................................................................................................49

### When to Completely Let Go of an Addict ............................................49

## Chapter 8 .................................................................................................................53

### Medical Treatment for an Addict in Recovery .....................................53

## Chapter 9 .................................................................................................................57

### Coping with the Death of an Addict .....................................................57

#### Processing the Premature Death of your Loved One ...........................59

#### Rid yourself of Guilt and Blame ...........................................................60

## Chapter 10 ...............................................................................................................63

### Commonly Abused Substances ..............................................................63

#### Alcohol ..................................................................................................63

#### Marijuana (Cannabis) ...........................................................................66

#### Cocaine .................................................................................................69

#### Heroin ...................................................................................................72

### Conclusion ..............................................................................................75

### Where to Find More Information and Support ....................................77

# Introduction

Living with an addict is like living in a never-ending nightmare! They are trapped in a never-ending hell and everyone around them is voluntarily or involuntarily drawn into that same hell.

Addiction is disease rooted in deep psychological problems. Although all addicts have the same disease with similar symptoms, behind every addict is an individual with their own personal and private journey, their own secrets, their own fears, their own pain and their own story to tell.

There is a common perception that drug addiction stands apart from alcoholism. Alcohol is a drug and abuse of alcohol is an addiction; both alcohol and drug abuse are addictions to mind-altering substances.

There are factors that differentiate alcohol use from drug use, but for the purposes of this book we will combine the two and refer to substance abuse and addiction, including the abuse of alcohol and drugs in these terms.

Substance abuse and addiction is a worldwide problem that knows no age, intellect, class, race or social standing. Although addiction may be more prolific under certain socio-economic conditions, to think that the problem is limited to only certain sectors of the population is a total misconception.

The intention of this book is to give the reader a frank and honest insight into the disease of addiction. It is not a source of academic scientific or psychological information. It neither condones nor condemns the addict-mind and it takes full cognizance of the pain and destruction addicts bring on themselves as well as family, friends, employers and virtually any other person they come into contact with.

Detailed statistics have been omitted from this book for two reasons. The first is that this book is written to inform, guide and hopefully inspire addicts in active addiction (who are unlikely to want to read this book), addicts in recovery and the loved ones of addicts either in recovery or in active addiction.

The second reason that statistics have been omitted from this book is that the statistics for recovery from substance abuse are rather grim. Addicts in early recovery and loved ones of addicts are looking for genuine hope and inspiration and some of the statistics can be quite shocking. All addicts in early recovery are mentally and emotionally fragile and wracked with fear, guilt, shame, and self-doubt. For an addict in early recovery, to study or be shown these statistics can make them feel that trying to recover is just a waste of time. Recovery is never a waste of time; even attempting recovery after relapse is never a waste of time. Some addicts relapse multiple times after a brief stint in recovery, but they keep coming back to treatment centers to try again. Every relapse strengthens their desire to recover because they don't want to live the hell of addiction. The hold of some substances over an addict is very strong and very difficult to escape. Addicts who don't give up on recovery have the courage and humility to try again and again. They deserve support because many addicts can and do recover, and so can your loved one.

It must be clearly understood that no one can stop an addict from using; no amount of love, rejection, aggression or coercion will influence an addict in active addiction. The addict is the only person who can make the decision to come clean and sober. One of the worst things you can do is to lecture an addict on all the side-effects of substance abuse, tell them they could end up on the streets or in jail and that they will become society drop-outs, etc. Addiction is a disease that's symptoms include denial; self-denial and denial of anything they are told. Another symptom is deceit. They deceive themselves that they are in control, and they will say anything to deceive you.

Living with the disease of addiction is a personal choice, whatever the driving factors. Just as no one can force another person into addiction, no one can stop an addict from using! No one can influence an addict into abstinence. The hold of addiction over an addict is very strong once an addict has become a regular user, and the longer an addict stays in active addiction the greater the hold. This hold is not only psychological but physiological as well.

Only if an addict fully accepts that they have a substance abuse problem, accepts full responsibility for their problem and admits that they are powerless over the hold the substance has over them can the recovery process begin. Only then will an addict be willing to listen to reason!

Recovery from addiction requires total personal surrender to the problem without any reservations. It takes extreme courage for an addict to surrender without reservation because the fear of living without their drug can be overwhelming. The fear created by the mere thought of facing the world clean and sober can drive an addict right back into the clutches of addiction.

Many addicts will promise to change when faced with harsh consequences of their actions. It must be understood that the addict genuinely does want to change in that moment when the reality of the pain and harm they cause others, or themselves hits home. In that moment it genuinely does hit home! Unfortunately, unless they go into professional treatment immediately (which is often not possible) the withdrawal symptoms, as well as the demons in their mind, will have them using again within less than twenty-four hours.

Addicts fully know and understand their problem, it is the hold that the substance has over them that will make them renege on all promises and fall back to using again. To come clean and sober, addicts need professional help. To accept professional help they must admit that they are powerless over their substance abuse and surrender to their problem. If they come to that point of total surrender, professional help must be immediately available and rehabilitation centers often have waiting lists for admission.

A life of sobriety escapes many addicts and countless addicts worldwide die while still in the clutches of substance abuse and addiction. Long-term substance abuse can lead to an addict becoming totally dysfunctional, dropping out of mainstream life and turning to begging, crime and prostitution to survive.

There are also life-long functional addicts who manage to hide their addictions and live a life that on the surface appears to be normal. Unfortunately, if you scratch below the surface there will be a history of a breakdown in family values, personal values, and social values.

Many long-term functional addicts will eventually fall apart, often triggered by the loss of their family or job. These external pressures can either push an addict deeper into addiction or become their rock-bottom that forces them to a place of total surrender and into seeking professional help to find recovery.

No matter how long an addict has been clean and sober, they will always be an addict in recovery! Just like many physical diseases are never fully cleared from the body - they are only latent and in remission, so substance abuse can be triggered again at any point. An addict in recovery has to always remain vigilant of their thoughts, reactions to external pressures and permanently keep away from people and establishments associated with drug or alcohol use. Loved ones must keep this in mind too and not assume that once the addict has been clean and sober for a period of time that the family can all go out together to the pub for a drink, or celebrate festive occasions with an alcoholic toast. One single alcoholic drink (even if the addict's substance of choice was not alcohol) can push the addict over the line and back into addiction. Any mind altering substance can trigger the brain back into cravings again.

"One drink won't do any harm" does not apply to addicts in recovery, ever. One alcoholic drink is too many because it can lead to a thousand alcoholic drinks just not being enough!

Any addict who is genuinely in recovery will confirm without any reservations that they know they are always little more than a hairs-breadth away from relapse. Managing recovery becomes a life-long way of life for an addict who has experienced the miracle of recovery and wants to stay clean and sober. Total abstinence from any mind-altering substances must be a life-long commitment.

Any addict who has become clean and sober and started on the road to recovery but does not remain vigilant and dedicated to the recovery process will inevitably relapse when exposed to the right riggers of their addiction. Any addict who at any stage of recovery believes them-self to be 'cured' is a fool!

# Dedication

This book is dedicated to all addicts suffering from the disease of addiction, whether they are still in active addiction or in recovery. It is also dedicated to the people who love and care for the addict and endure extreme emotional pain and suffering as well, often at the hands of the addict or by standing by helplessly watching their loved one slowly self-destruct, often to the point of death.

### *We did not choose to become addicts!*

*When we were growing up, all of us had dreams. Every child has heard a relative or neighbor ask "What do you want to be when you grow up?" Even if some of us did not have elaborate dreams of success, most of us dreamed of work, families and a future of dignity and respect. But no one asked, "Do you want to be a drug addict when you grow up?"*

*We didn't choose to become addicts, and we cannot choose to stop being addicts. We have the disease of addiction. We are not responsible for having it, but we are responsible for our recovery. Having learned that we are sick people and that there is a way to recovery, we can move away from blaming circumstances, or ourselves and we can move into living the solution. We didn't choose addiction, but we can choose recovery.*

### *Just for today: I choose recovery!*

Copyright © Narcotics Anonymous Just for Today Meditations

Reprinted by permission of NA World Services, Inc. All rights reserved

# Chapter 1

# Understanding Addiction

Addiction is a complicated disease of the mind that results in self-destruction. In the self-destruction process, an addict becomes a toxic core drawing family, loved ones, friends and even employers into their ever-increasing spiral of pain, abuse, destruction, and dysfunction.

Often the gravitation towards the addict's self-destructive lifestyle by family, loved ones and friends is unintentional and goes virtually unnoticed as people surrounding the addict try to understand and rationalize the changes in behavior, emergence of deception, belligerence, aggression and the gradual transition of a well-loved person into an almost evil stranger.

Employers are negatively affected by having an unreliable employee on their hands. This can affect the morale of other staff and negatively impact productivity.

In some countries, an employee cannot be dismissed for poor work performance if it is established that the employee is an addict in active addiction. The employee has to be afforded the opportunity to get professional treatment at a recovery center. When the employee returns to work after a stint in a recovery center (as an in or out-patient) and their work performance remains poor, only then does the employer have grounds for dismissal. Some addicts do return clean and sober beginning the road to recovery and start delivering work of an acceptable level.

## Defining a Drug Addict and an Alcoholic

The Merriam-Webster dictionary defines drug addiction as: "Compulsive need for and use of a habit-forming substance characterized by tolerance and well-defined physiological symptoms upon withdrawal; broadly - persistent compulsive use of a substance known to the user to be harmful."

The Merriam-Webster dictionary defines alcoholism as "a chronic, progressive, potentially fatal disorder marked by excessive and usually compulsive drinking of alcohol leading to psychological and physical dependence or addiction."

Both of these definitions are a brief and clinical description of a compulsive human behavior that ultimately will lead the user to self-harm. The reality is that both drug addicts and alcoholics abuse mind-altering substances that they know are harmful to themselves mentally and physically. Both alcohol and drugs are addictive; both substances render the user unable to control their compulsion to continue using their substance of choice!

Substance abuse is a far-reaching, deep-rooted personal problem that degenerates into a disease of the mind, eventually causing physical illness. All addicts' lifestyle gradually bleeds its toxicity into the lives of people around them, especially family and friends.

Drug addicts will go to extreme lengths to hide their problem from family and friends because drug addiction carries a social stigma and is illegal. Drug addicts will use alone or with like-minded people, but always in secret. This deceptive behavior often leaves people around the addict confused, desperate and troubled as they try to make sense of the changes in the addict's personality and what they see and experience at the hands of the addict! Reality is that no drug addict will have the nerve to say "I'm just going to stop at the crack-house to smoke-up or shoot-up with my friends!"

Alcoholics can be more open because alcohol is a socially accepted drug. In many instances, it is deemed sophisticated, social or fun-loving to drink alcohol. People who prefer not to drink alcohol are often pressurized and belittled in social situations. Being drunk is 'cool' and 'having a great night out'. Alcoholics openly say "I'm just going to stop at the pub and have a few drinks with my friends!" Alcohol is a socially accepted legal drug.

The alcoholic beverage industry is worth billions worldwide. Alcohol is repeatedly marketed to millions of people daily. All marketing depicts happy people or sophisticated people drinking their brand of alcohol. The reality of alcohol addiction is side-lined. No mention is made that alcohol is an addictive substance that can lead to mental and social dysfunction, crime and even death. That alcohol not only destroys the addict but very often their families as well.

Many countries have introduced laws forcing tobacco products to carry a very clear warning on the packaging that smoking tobacco can cause lung cancer, emphysema and other disorders of the respiratory system. Smokers are made to sit in a 'smoking section' in restaurants and other public places. This is of course very good because tobacco is a harmful substance and can also cause respiratory problems for non-smokers if they inhale tobacco smoke. This is termed passive smoking or second-hand smoking. Tobacco is not a mind-altering substance, it causes a physical addiction. It does not incite aggression, violence or dysfunction. It does not destroy families either and it has become almost the norm for smokers not to smoke inside their house, but rather in their garden if a partner objects or if they have children.

The irony of this is that tobacco products are strictly controlled by laws and regulations, drugs are illegal and can lead to criminal prosecution, but alcohol that is the most commonly abused mind-altering substance worldwide that leads to family and social dysfunction, the potential death not only of the user but of innocent people and destroys the lives of countless people is viewed as socially acceptable, and even desirable.

Both drugs and alcohol are mind-altering, habit-forming substances! The devastation caused by dependency to any of these substances on the addict and those around them is exactly the same!

## What Causes Addiction?

There is much debate around studies and findings that some people are genetically predisposed to addiction. Although science has not yet identified candidate genes that can be directly linked to addiction, multiple studies conducted on addicts and non-addicts have shown an average 50% genetic predisposition to substance or behavioral addictions.

All humans and animals have an evolutionary genetic predisposition to addiction that relates to feeding and through feeding to the survival of each species. The purpose is for humans and animals to find foods that they like and that make them feel good (healthy). The advantage to associating pleasure with food means that humans and animals would continue searching for those foods to sustain a healthy life.

Although this genetic predisposition to addiction and survival served humans at a primal level, and humans have long since evolved beyond basic survival, the human brain is still pre-programmed for addiction. This genetic programming does not, however, doom everyone to substance or behavioral addictions.

There are also external factors that play a major role in predisposition to addiction. These include:

- Children of addicts are at a high risk of becoming addicts themselves

- A family history of addiction (even if parents were not addicts) increases the risk of addiction

- Children who are not taught proper coping skills

- Children who suffer childhood trauma that is never dealt with

- Trauma or abuse at any stage in life that is not addressed and dealt with

- Stress in adolescence and peer-pressure

- Ongoing daily family-related stress such as domestic violence, extended financial issues, etc

- Acute stress related to major life changes like death of a loved one or divorce

- Loneliness and social isolation through circumstance or through a personal inability to socialize

Predisposition to addiction is a combination of genetics and poor coping skills. People who have a low genetic predisposition to addiction could evolve into full-blown addicts if they use mind-altering substances to medicate emotional pain or escape domestic or social circumstances. Mind altering substances affect brain chemistry; all addictions are processed from the same part of the brain. Repeated intake of mind-altering substances will begin to reprogram the brain. Even if initially taken in small amounts, the stimulation of the pleasure/reward response system in the brain compels the person to begin chasing the high, the relaxation, the elevated energy level or confidence effect of the substance. Simultaneously, the body and brain begin to develop a tolerance for the substance. This leads to higher and higher daily intake to experience the same effect until the person can no longer function properly without using. They have then fallen into active addiction.

Whatever the dynamics around why someone initially begins to abuse mind-altering substances, addiction is a disease. Much like type 2 Diabetes, cardiac disease and other similar diseases that are a combination of genetic predisposition and an unhealthy lifestyle, addiction comprises the same combination. People with type 2 Diabetes or cardiac disease are not shunned by family and society on diagnosis and with the proper medical intervention and lifestyle changes they can lead healthy lives and remain active members of society.

Unfortunately, addiction is cloaked by shame and disgrace. Families are ashamed to admit that their loved one is an addict. Addicts are ashamed to seek help so they try to heal themselves and fall further into addiction. Society needs to recognize addiction as a disease. A treatable disease that with the right medical and professional intervention, ongoing treatment and a change in the addict's mindset and lifestyle can help the addict break the destructive cycle of addiction, return to sobriety, re-enter mainstream life and once again become an active member of society.

# Chapter 2

# Identifying Addiction

The word 'addict' carries a shameful social stigma and people do not want to identify themselves or a family member as an addict for fear of social disapproval and rejection. Both addicts and family members are often well aware of the situation, are living the hell and the downward spiral, but will refuse to acknowledge the problem because of fear and shame. The problem becomes shrouded in secrecy where it grows cloaked in silence. This type of attitude towards addiction is what creates a cycle of shame and addiction that follows from one generation to the next.

Drug abuse does not only imply addiction to hard-core narcotics. Drug abuse includes addiction to off-the-shelf and over-the-counter drugs, prescription drugs, nitrous oxide, intoxicating fumes found is in many adhesives, and other less common herbal and plant extracts.

It is very common for people to become addicted to prescription drugs unintentionally such as tranquilizers and pain medication. Initially, the drug treats the symptoms or source of physical pain, but with that, there is also a high that alters the users' state of mind in what is perceived to be a positive way. It can be a great sense of comfort, release of stress, a warm feeling of drowsiness that leads to a peaceful period of dreamless sleep or any experience that makes the user feel 'better' mentally and emotionally.

The user continues to use the medication even after the initial symptoms being treated have healed because they are now chasing the high. This can be a gradual process that goes almost unnoticed by the user until they realize that even when they want to stop taking the medication, they are unable to. They have now become addicted.

## What you Need to Know about Addict Behaviour

The points listed below are symptomatic behaviors of substance abusers. Although they may not all be recognizable traits in your loved one's lifestyle because addicts are so adept at deceit, these points may shed some light on aspects of their behavior that you are unable to fathom. Once these thinking patterns have set in, you can accept your loved one's substance abuse is out of control and their substance of choice now controls them.

An addict in active addiction is unlikely to be willing to read through this list, but you can possibly go through the list of points together if you can approach them in a more sober moment and get their honest cooperation. If they are honest and acknowledge the fact that they are actively using substances you must encourage them to agree to professional help as soon as possible. If there is not swift professional intervention nothing will change. In an altered mood, later on, they may completely deny that they agreed to the list of points and call you a liar. Laying blame is a voracious symptom of the addict-mind; they refuse to accept personal responsibility!

If you are unable to elicit any cooperation from your loved one but need to have your suspicions confirmed, you will have to keep the list of points at hand and do some investigation of your own. If you live together with other family members who are old enough to be concerned and discuss the problem with you, bring them in. See if you can definitely identify any of the points on the list.

- Addicts turn to drugs or alcohol when experiencing even slight emotional pain or stress

- Addicts do sometimes think that they may have a substance abuse problem and it does concern them, but they are powerless to control it

- Addicts think about their substance of choice almost all of the time, obsessing over when they will use it next, and how much they could use if they had more money.

- Addicts always ensure that they have enough of their substance of choice available, making provision for holiday's away (stockpiling), festive occasions, etc.

- Addicts panic severely if they think that they may run out of their substance of choice

- Addicts place buying their substance of choice before buying other daily necessities

- Addicts become defensive if anyone mentions or asks them about their substance use

- Addicts lie to other people about how much drugs or alcohol they use in a day

- Addicts can secretly feel guilty or ashamed when using drugs or alcohol but will not admit it

- Addicts often need to use drugs or alcohol after waking up or before going to sleep to get them through the day and to fall asleep at night

- Addicts firmly believe that their substance of choice is a necessity in their life and they will go to any length to ensure that they get what they need

- Addicts do secretly try to avoid their substance of choice, especially once they realize that it is controlling their life; without professional help, they cannot stop

- Addicts commonly use one substance to overcome the effects of another

- Addicts work or educational performance always suffers because of their substance use

- Addicts generally lose or avoid friends they knew when they were clean and sober because of their substance use

- Addicts regularly feign illness to get a doctor's prescription, often studying symptoms of illnesses that would require the substance they want

- Addicts always suffer from dramatic mood-swings and often secretly question their sanity

- Addicts constantly have people asking or commenting on changes in their behavior or personality; too many questions can result in them avoiding certain people

- Addicts sleeping or eating patterns are almost always impacted by their substances use; excessive sleeping or going without sleep for days, and mostly loss of appetite

- Addicts always keep secret stashes of their substance hidden so that they can use alone if they want or need to

If you recognize any of these behavioral traits, your loved one is undoubtedly an addict. It does not matter how much or how little they may be using, once any substance starts to control their thinking and alters their life patterns, they are an addict!

## Further Identifying a Loved One as an Addict

If you have gone through the points listed above without your loved one's cooperation and suspect that they fell into active addiction, don't expect that if you confront them directly with your suspicions they will admit it to you. Expect denial, defensiveness, outrage and even aggression at your questions. Some addicts know that they are addicted and others are in denial, but either way, your questions will be viewed as prying and will not be welcome!

If you want to further clarify your suspicions you will have to observe their behavior for typical outward signs of addiction. These include:

- Uncharacteristic irritability, combative behavior or aggression

- Uncontrolled giggling, laughing, euphoria, talkativeness followed misery or falling asleep

- Daily mood swings from euphoria to depression - four seasons in one day, every day

- Loss of interest in mixing with family and friends

- Loss of interest in activities and hobbies that were previously important to them

- Money or items of value inexplicably disappearing

- Constantly asking for money or loans (that generally are not repaid)

- Stories of being mugged to explain missing valuables like a mobile phone, tablet or laptop but refusing to put in a police report

- Unexplained absences from home, sometimes for days

- Defensiveness when asked where they've been

- Lying about their whereabouts

- Isolating themselves in their bedroom and keeping the door locked

- Sleeping like the dead for hours on end and waking up depressed and moody

- Loss of appetite, turning meals away and weight loss

- Loss of interest in personal appearance and hygiene

- Change in complexion; either very pale or flushed

- Developing a scabby skin and constant scratching (depending on type of drug used)

- Sudden onset of regular nosebleeds or easily bruising (depending on the type of drug used)

- Tooth discoloration and decay (depending on the type of drugs used)

- Blisters on the palms of the hands, fingers, and lips (depending on the type of drugs used)

- Bloodshot eyes, puffy eyes, dilated or constricted pupils

## How to Approach the Subject of Addiction

As mentioned earlier don't think that anyone, no matter how close your relationship, is just going to come out and admit that they are an addict. Even if they admit that they use any substance, particularly alcohol or marijuana (which is gaining social acceptance), they will tell you that they know what they are doing and are in full control of their using. Even if you can see otherwise, your approach will not be met with a positive reaction.

Depending on the relationship you have with the addict, the dynamics of the living environment, etc you could be met with calm denial and reassurance (manipulation), or you could be met with outright aggressive denial that could lead to assault if there is a dynamic of domestic violence or flight where the addict will leave and not return. If it is a friendship, you may not see your friend again for a very long time, if ever. If it is a family member they could stay away for a number of days.

Family dynamics play an important role in confronting an addict. If the family has a history of addiction, there could be confrontation, finger-pointing and laying blame. The situation can even evolve into physical violence. Children who have been raised in homes where substance abuse is prevalent are not taught proper life and coping skills so they have a natural predisposition to substance abuse. This is not only because they have been surrounded by family members who abuse substances, but because they regard substances as a means of coping with daily life pressures.

Often parents who are or were addicts don't want their children to fall into the same destructive and aimless lifestyle. Even if they have become clean and sober, they may not realize that in the years that they were in active addiction they failed to teach their child or children proper life and coping skills. Unless the whole family goes into therapy after the parent has gone through a rehabilitation process, their children will still be negatively affected by the improper way they were raised.

Many recovering addicts overlook this very real factor! They go through the rehabilitation process, remain dedicated to their recovery and are eager to make up for the years that they lost with their children. They genuinely want to create loving family homes and spend quality time with their children, but much psychological damage is done to children of using addicts.

Psychological damage suffered by neglected babies, toddlers, small children through to teens leave deep mental and emotional scars as well as wrongful thinking patterns that people don't realize. This leads to psychological problems in adulthood, ranging from minor issues to severe issues that can render the child of an addict totally unable to function properly in society. Most children of addicts will seek relief from their emotional pain in substances, repeating the cycle of substance abuse.

If the family has no history of addiction, confronting an addict about your concerns will be met with denial. Lies, shifting blame and accusations turned onto you or the family are common. You could even be left feeling guilty and regretful after the addict's denial; all addicts become master manipulators.

Either way, you will have to do whatever it takes to confirm if your loved one is abusing a substance or substances. This is even more important if you are living together - if the addict is your husband, wife, partner or child. Mind altering substances change the user from someone you know and love, to a total stranger who can put your household at risk through their deceptive, manipulative and sometimes even criminal behavior.

# Chapter 3

# Treatment and Finding Sobriety

## Planned Interventions

There are currently a number of television programs on intervention by family and friends of addicts to encourage the addict to agree to get professional help to find sobriety and go into recovery. It is always debatable whether programs like these are staged or not.

Either way, it is not advisable to try to plan an intervention for a friend or loved one in active addiction on your own. Addiction is a very complicated, self-centered disease and every addict is an individual with their own thoughts and personality, so what you have seen on television might not work out in the same way.

Interventions can sometimes succeed, but they can also go horribly wrong leaving people who staged the intervention with life-long regrets. Many addicts will feel that they have been betrayed if unknowingly led into an intervention situation as they are in the television programs. This feeling of betrayal can lead to acts of violence towards the people present, the addict breaking all family ties and taking to the streets, the addict fleeing the situation an taking an overdose and in so doing committing suicide intentionally or unintentionally and many other unpleasant scenarios.

Being unexpectedly faced by a room full of people all focusing on the addict and telling the addict how much they are loved and how sad everyone feels seeing the addict self-destruct can be overwhelming for most addicts. Being self-centered in thought, the addict's guilt (yes, most addicts carry a lot of guilt) could become overwhelming. With their poor coping skills, the overwhelmed and guilt-ridden addict could turn the situation around and start blaming family and friends. Deceit and lies are an addicts tools, manipulation their survival. It is not unheard of for an addict to accuse innocent people of horrors like rape, molestation, etc sowing seeds of doubt and suspicion within the family circle. The addict will do this to get the focus taken off them, and the addict will do this without conscience!

Remember, substance abuse alters the user's brain and thinking patterns. Rational thinking does not exist in the addict mind. Impulsive, self-centered and irrational thought patterns dominate! Addicts become very self-absorbed and their lives revolve around only their needs, getting their next high, coming down and then using again. This excludes anyone and everyone else's needs, even their own children's.

An addict's prime focus is on getting their substance to use and their sole interest is in their own need to use! This focus on their need to use and getting their next high is so strong that it even overrides the inborn human instinct of survival. Addicts place their lives on the line time and again without any contemplation of the fact!

If you want to stage an intervention it must be very carefully planned. You must plan the intervention with the help of a professional social worker, drug counselor or psychologist. Present at the intervention must be only direct family, close friends and the professional who is directing the intervention.

You must also ensure beforehand that you have made provision at a rehabilitation center to admit the addict immediately should they agree to go into treatment. It will be of no use if you still have to take the time to book a bed at a rehabilitation center after the addict has agreed. Many centers have waiting lists. Even the slightest delay will most likely cause the addict to change their mind.

If the addict declines going into treatment at an intervention but change their mind a few days later and you cannot find an available bed at a rehabilitation center you can try your local hospital's psychiatric ward. If there is a bed available they may admit an addict and go through the withdrawal and detoxification process with them, which must be done under medical supervision. The detoxification process lasts for about seventy-two hours, which is also the time period in which the addict's life can be endangered from the effects of chemical withdrawal. The addict will require controlled medication for some time afterward. Psychiatric wards will often keep the addict as an in-patient until a bed becomes available at a rehabilitation center. Psychiatric wards also have resident psychologists and psychiatrists who can offer the addict support while they are there.

It is not advised that the professional that you ask to manage the intervention process is affiliated with any religion. All addicts in active addiction have an innate rejection of religion and anything affiliated with religion. If the addict is preached to from a religious perspective including sinfulness and hell and damnation, your intervention is almost guaranteed to fail and could have calamitous repercussions! The substances become the addicts' god, and all addicts exist in a spiritual void.

## Gradual Grooming

If an addict has a very close relationship with a parent, sibling, friend, spouse, partner or even their own child gradually grooming the addict into acknowledging that their substance abuse has become out of control and their life has become unmanageable can be successful. For it to be successful the relationship must be a long-standing relationship and there must be a high degree of mutual trust in the relationship.

The 'grooming' must be well thought through and you must only address the problem of addiction when it is appropriate. If you begin to nag at the addict every time they see you they will most likely switch-off and begin to avoid you.

The first thing you must do before you open any line of recovery conversation is to educate yourself on substance abuse and addiction. You must put your own beliefs, prejudices, and attitudes aside. Only an addict will ever be able to understand what another addict goes through in active addiction! You may not understand the complicated dynamics of addiction, but if you want to bring the addict into recovery, you probably love the addict very much. Love and understanding are enough for you to begin your process of 'grooming'.

Again, you must ensure that there is a rehabilitation center that has an open bed before you speak to the addict, just in case the addict suddenly agrees with you and is open to seeking professional help.

Make sure that the addict is quite relaxed and not openly high or coming down from a high when you broach the subject. Test the waters by gently touching on the subject of their substance abuse and gauge their response. If the response is immediately confrontational, the time is not right. If they are open to the conversation, encourage them to discuss their lifestyle with you. Avoid judging and preaching at all costs! Even if they disclose something that you find quite shocking, the conversation must be collaborative for it to be successful.

Speak with kindness and express your concerns about the dangers of their lifestyle. Let them know that your concerns are founded on your love for them and let them know that if they are willing to seek professional help you will support them.

- Don't confront the addict with condemnation to encourage them to seek help. Don't judge or blame them for past and present situations and wrongs. Don't bring religion into the conversation at all. The disease of addiction, unfortunately, rejects any godliness!

- If the addict indicates that they would like to become clean and sober but they are very afraid of life without their drug (when in active addiction the thought of living without your drug is genuinely terrifying), reassure them that you will support them through the process and afterward. Confirm that rehabilitation centers administer drugs to ease the symptoms of withdrawal and to ease the cravings after detoxification.

If the addict has had their children removed by welfare, owes large sums of money to people or anything similar, avoid these issues at this stage. Gentle, kind encouragement may just be the catalyst that gets the addict into a rehabilitation center.

## Rehabilitation Centres and Half-Way Houses

If an intervention has been successful it will only succeed in the long-run if the addict has agreed to be admitted as an inpatient at a rehabilitation center. If in the intervention the addict refused to be admitted to a rehabilitation center, but agrees to get them-self clean and makes a hundred other promises, crosses their heart and hopes to die if they do not keep their word, your intervention has failed. All addicts need professional help!

The addict will not die from not keeping their word to all involved in the intervention, but they do stand a good chance of dying from the consequences of their substance abuse.

Because mind-altering substances have the potential to re-program the brain, active addiction severely affects an addict's thought patterns. Addicts become increasingly self-absorbed to the exclusion of other all peoples' needs, considerations or the addict's responsibility to them (for example babies and children), and the addict's life becomes totally unmanageable. Much emphasis in treatment focuses on psychotherapy, occupational therapy to get the addict re-involved in life and also becoming involved with support groups like Alcoholics Anonymous and Narcotics Anonymous. Family support during treatment plays an important role.

Most addicts will need extensive in-patient treatment at a rehabilitation center. The minimum inpatient treatment recommended is around a month, but addicts can remain in in-patient facilities for up to about four months.

There are also outpatient treatment programs available, but these would only be recommended for functioning addicts who are employed and on the surface appear to lead a normal life. These addicts have not yet fallen into total dysfunction, but still, require professional treatment to heal and find recovery.

Addicts who find sobriety and have begun their journey towards recovery in a rehabilitation center are often advised to move into a halfway-house when leaving the rehabilitation center to allow for a gradual re-integration with mainstream society. The half-way house controls much of the addicts' daily routine, similar to life in the rehabilitation center. Addicts are encouraged to, and often assisted in finding employment. There are set times for waking up, if unemployed, an addict is assigned daily tasks around the half-way house like housekeeping, preparing meals or gardening. Meal times set and there is a night-time curfew. All addicts must ensure that they are home before curfew.

Regular drug tests are conducted and group therapy through regular meetings at Alcoholics Anonymous or Narcotics Anonymous is a must-do. The halfway-house is system is designed to reinforce the coping skills that the addicts have learned at the rehabilitation center and to once again introduce self-discipline, rational thinking, responsibility, and routine into the addicts' lives. They are also able to rebuild their self-esteem and self-confidence in a protective environment where professional support is readily available if they find themselves feeling fragile. Half-way houses function in tandem with rehabilitation centers and are highly recommended so that the addict is strong and confident when they leave to face life on their own again.

In all recovery through rehabilitation and half-way house centers can take up to a year of full time controlled professional treatment. A year is a very small price to pay to gain a lifetime of sobriety.

Recovery from addiction is a gradual process that requires life-long dedication and maintenance by the recovering addict to prevent relapse. Recovery is not a once-off spectacular event that leads to instant sobriety!

It takes a tremendous amount of courage to admit to being an addict! To do that is to admit to being a failure, an undesirable and a derelict by society's standards. How other people may or may not judge an addict in recovery who has admitted their disease is beyond any ones control. Finding sobriety and long-term recovery is all that matters. By encouraging your loved one to take personal responsibility they will begin to regain control of their life and begin to live again.

Living the life of an addict in active addiction is living a life of endless hell; living the life of the walking dead! Living the life of an addict in recovery is living a life of gratitude where freedom from addiction brings great joy and appreciation for even the smallest things in life. When you have lived a life trapped in the deepest darkness that can exist, finding freedom from that entrapment brings a genuine love for life, gratitude, and humility.

## Long- Term Recovery

Family, friends and loved ones must be realistic about their expectations of long-term recovery for any addict. Worldwide statistics show that on average 50% of addicts who go into treatment centers will relapse into active addiction at some point in the future.

The longer they stay in a rehabilitation center and a half-way house, the better the chances of the addict staying clean and sober, but it is still no guarantee. Pressures of mainstream life, poor coping skills, getting back with a partner or spouse who is still in active addiction, low self-esteem, and a judgmental environment are only some of the factors that can push an addict back into active addiction.

Also not using the coping skills and tools that they were equipped with while in treatment, not attending support group meetings a number of times a week and not working on maintaining sobriety can lead to a resurgence of the addict mind and thought patterns, and back to active addiction.

Is it worth having an addict admitted to a rehabilitation center again after a relapse; is there any hope of recovery? Most certainly! If there is a desire to become clean and sober, there is always hope. Many addicts only achieve sobriety and long-term recovery after a number of stints in rehabilitation. As mentioned before, addiction is a very complicated and deep-rooted disease of the mind. Relapse is a breakdown in the mind's thought patterns, the resurgence of wrongful thinking. Re-programming an addict's brain can take a number of attempts and hundreds of hours of psychotherapy - but if the will is there, it is always worth trying again.

Unfortunately, the statistics of a 50% relapse rate is based on information of addicts admitted for in or out-patient recovery programs. There are many, many more addicts who never agree to go into any recovery program and are therefore are not included in statistics.

Because of the stigma attached to drug addiction, in particular, there is little sympathy for an addict who dies. Many will say they got what they deserved!

Alcohol-related deaths are often not attributed to the underlying alcoholism and recorded and liver or kidney failure as well as cardiac disease.

The number of lives lost worldwide as a result of substance abuse is not accurately known, but substance abuse destroys the lives of millions of beautiful, highly intelligent, kind, loving, caring and generous souls who became caught up in the dance with death. The dance between mind-altering substances and human beings!

# Chapter 4

# Enabling and Co-Dependency

There is a very fine line between supporting an addict and enabling an addict. Co-dependent relationships are also easily formed. Enablers and co-dependents are most commonly parents, children, a spouse or partner.

## Enabling

An addict finds an enabler in someone who actually supports and encourages their dysfunctional behavior. The enabler believes that they are protecting the addict from the consequences of their lifestyle, but in fact, their actions encourage the addict to sink further into addiction. They believe they are doing this out of love for the addict, which may hold some truth, but their love for the addict becomes their own, and addict's downfall. Enablers learn to accept the unacceptable and blur the boundaries between right and wrong. They will lie on behalf of the addict or cover for them at work or school by calling in to report the addict as ill when in fact they are suffering from the effects of substances or gone missing-in-action on a drinking or drug binge.

This cycle of protecting the addict from facing the consequences of their self-destructive lifestyle has the opposite effect to protecting the addict in the long-term. The more the addict gets away with, the further the addict will push the boundaries of their substance abuse.

The addict learns to rely on the enabler, often believing that they are entitled to the enablers support and protection. The enabler becomes completely caught up in the addict's lifestyle, often putting their own needs, health and welfare at risk to support and protect the addict. The enabler's emotional needs and physical wellbeing are of little or no interest to the addict because addicts are completely self-absorbed. Addicts are incapable of caring while in active addiction!

The addict's self-absorption generally leads to the enabler being subjected to verbal, mental or emotional abuse. It can even include physical abuse like slapping, pushing and shoving. In some instances, the physical abuse can escalate to include assault or threaten the enabler with a dangerous weapon. Because addicts want their own way and always want instant gratification, abuse becomes a factor when the enabler begins to resist or is genuinely unable to meet the addict's demands. The stronger the enabler stands their ground against the addict, the more they expose themselves to the addict's obsessions with getting what they want. They can place themselves in mortal danger by resisting the addict and by the false belief that this person that they love and who has always loved them will not harm them. Wrong! The addict is no longer the person they once knew. In active addiction you are always dealing with the drug and not the person. The substance controls the addict. The person they once loved is no longer the same person, they are enslaved to their substance of choice; their substance of choice controls them.

Are you an enabler? Do you -

- Regularly give the addict money?

- Pay the addicts debts or re-pay the addict's loans?

- Do you cover for the addict when they are unable to meet their personal responsibilities?

- Do you lie for the addict if their behavior has led to other people asking questions?

- Do you accept the unacceptable regarding the addict's behavior?

- Do you trivialize serious issues and sweep matters under the carpet?

- Do you pay for the addict's food, bills, childcare costs or rent even when you can't afford to?

- Do you pay the addict's fines to keep them from facing the consequences of non-payment?

- Do you know that the addict is stealing money or items from you but avoid confrontation?

- Do you apologize or make amends on behalf of the addict?

If you are an enabler, you must seek professional help and support. You are not responsible for your loved one's drug problem. By protecting them from facing the consequences of their lifestyle you are not helping them. By facing the consequences of their dysfunctional lifestyle and being forced to take responsibility for their actions, the addict stands a better chance of opting for recovery through their suffering by their own deeds.

For the most part, enablers have some level of psychological problems themselves. It could stem from many past issues in their life ranging from fear, or a dysfunctional childhood that left them without proper coping skills, to having had a parent who enabled a spouse or child. Whether the addict opts for recovery or rejects recovery, it is always advised that the addict and the enabler be separated for both of their sake. The enabler must seek professional counseling and strengthen them-self through attending support groups to deal with guilt and detachment issues.

The enabler must also learn to put their own needs, health, and welfare first. They must re-build their self-confidence, self-esteem and learn to enjoy life again.

Under professional guidance the enabler will be educated on the causes of substance abuse, the behavior of addicts and the Three C's that anyone close to an addict must understand - you did not Cause it; you cannot Cure it; you cannot Control it!

## Co-Dependency

What sets co-dependency apart from enabling? Co-dependents display addict behavior. Addiction is not only reserved to abusing substances. It also includes obsessive, compulsive behavior patterns and actions, and the cause of this is also rooted in deep-set psychological problems.

A co-dependent on the surface wants to save the addict, but beneath the surface, there are many and wide-ranging issues that spurn them on like insecurity, control, power and even ego. As with many psychological issues, the co-dependent may be totally unaware of the subconscious issues that plague them.

To briefly touch on the four underlying psychological issues mentioned:

Insecurity in a relationship leads to a need to be sure that your partner or child will never leave. In partner relationships, this could be triggered by past experiences and fear of abandonment. In partner relationships, an insecure co-dependent may be subjected to severe abuse by the addict, but they will continue to support them, 'love' them and try to cure them because they believe that they cannot live without the addict. In parent/child relationships the parent may fear not having anyone to look after and nurture anymore; the fear of the 'empty nest syndrome'.

Control ties in with insecurity in any relationship." You cannot leave me if I am in control of you!"

Power is partly connected to insecurity and control, but it also implies that if the co-dependent has control over everything that the addict has in life, the addict is effectively unable to exist without the support of the co-dependent.

In relationships of power and control the abuse may be reversed, with the co-dependent excerpting their power and control on the addict, often placing the addict's life in danger if they try to break free. Examples are a man who pimps his drug-addicted partner, older (mainly male) 'lovers' who prey on young male and female addicts who mostly come from the streets. These types of relationships continue with the addict being exposed to often extreme abuse, but they stay because they are being kept off the streets and are given drugs on a regular basis.

Ego, the false self, thrives on the fact that the addict cannot survive without them. They also often portray a long-suffering image to the outer world to garner compliments of how good a person they are. In these cases, the addict may also be subjected to abuse behind closed doors.

These are only some of the psychological issues that lie behind co-dependency, and the examples given are mere guidelines of what may be driving the co-dependent. Codependents are behavioral addicts, ranging from desperate to very dangerous. All co-dependents need professional help but few will ever seek it because their problem is a behavioral addiction and they are unable to identify with that concept.

BIELLA BLOM

# Chapter 5

# What if the Addict is a Minor?

Peer pressure plays a major role in minors being drawn into substance abuse. Another obvious influence is children that come from homes where substance abuse is the norm. These children will often spurn other children on and invite them home, where underage drinking or smoking marijuana is not frowned upon.

There are a number of changes that parents will notice in their child's behavior that may give rise to suspicion of substance abuse. These would be the same as listed in Chapter 2 of this book under the sub-heading 'Further Identifying a Loved One as an Addict'. In addition to the points listed, with minors you can also include:

- A change in the way they dress (could indicate gang affiliation or group identification)

- A change in the way they speak and terms they use (again gang or group related)

- A sudden change in the type of music they listen to

- A change in their circle of friends; rejecting long-standing friends

- Rejection of siblings; not wanting siblings to go out with them anymore

- Rejection of any type of authority

Children are generally first introduced to 'soft' drugs like alcohol and marijuana. Not every child that tries different substances will become an addict. Many people find the mind-altering effects of substances very unpleasant, and in some people, even a small amount can cause them to become very ill which will put them off completely.

The danger of 'soft' drugs is that it lowers a person's inhibitions and makes them more open to suggestion. This can lead to trying harder drugs and becoming addicted to hard drugs. We live in a society driven by media influences, consumerism, commercialism and instant transfer of information. This has created an environment where there are social rules of what is 'in' and what is 'out'. Most people are caught up in this trap of how to look, what to do, where to be, etc - and that includes millions of people worldwide who have been clean and sober all their lives.

The problem with this lifestyle is that we try to live up to what and who we think we should be and shy away from what and who we really are. We lose touch with our true self and forget where we come from while trying to impress the world and post everything on social media. Minors are no different and they want to identify and be accepted. The social pressures placed on society at large by media influences can imprint heavily on the immature and susceptible mind of an adolescent. If they feel that they do not meet the standards of social acceptability, they could go out and seek acceptance elsewhere.

If a minor identifies and is accepted by a certain group (including gangs), they will do what it takes to try and mold them-self into what is acceptable. It can create severe stress to constantly live up to what they should be and not what they are. Substances often make this constant living behind a mask a bit easier.

If you are the parent of a child who comes from a solid and stable loving home environment where proper values have been instilled, it can come as a great shock to you to realize that your child is abusing substances. Because of the social stigma attached to drug use, in particular, your initial reaction could be an over-reaction. Denial, blame, disappointment, anger, and retribution! None of these thoughts and emotions will solve the problem, so just calm down! Give yourself and the rest of your family some time to think and take in the problem. Don't make rash decisions on the spur of the moment. Do immediately seek professional advice so that you can be guided and educated on what steps to take.

Be aware that depending on your child's state of mind, predisposition to addiction and the family dynamics, you could all be in for a very rough ride that could last for years!

The major difference between the effect substances have when first used by minors as opposed to when first used in adulthood is the effect it has on brain chemistry. There are many studies that have confirmed that the changes in brain chemistry and the programming of the brain tends to be more severe and indelible when substances are used by young teens, as opposed to the effect it will have on an adult brain.

Studies have shown that people who begin to use mind-altering substances in their early to mid teens will find it more difficult to break the addiction. Even if they do break the addiction and become clean and sober, they may suffer from severe depression and even psychosis throughout their lives, making the avoidance of mind-altering substances very challenging.

Once everyone has calmed down and you educated yourself a bit on the problems associated the substance abuse and addiction, you need to sit down with your child and have a frank and open discussion. If you intend raving and ranting and laying down the law, don't even bother having a discussion because your attitude could do more harm than good.

Approach the problem with empathy and understanding. You are the adult is the discussion, so you should have the maturity to take the lead with firm kindness. You could be met with anything from tears and denial to belligerence. Handle it! You are trying to understand how this happened and to what degree your child is using substances. You want to build trust and hope to get honest answers in return. Is your child still in the experimental stage, or have they already progressed to active addiction? Their response to you could be a good indicator. If they are still in the experimental stage, they will probably be more receptive and communicate more freely. If they are already in active addiction, they will be more inclined to avoid open communication, opting rather for deceit or aggression to get rid of you.

Definitely, don't make a pact with your child that you will support them and together as a family you will solve their addiction problem. No one can 'love' and addict into sobriety! All addicts need professional help, and the sooner they get professional help and are open to accepting professional help, the better their chances of coming clean and sober and going into recovery.

The best you can do is to remove your child from the friends that they are associating with and have your child admitted to a rehabilitation center that deals specifically with minors. As the parent of an underage child you can do that, but do it with kindness. Explain why you are taking the action that you are. Reassure them that you are doing it out of love for them and not to punish them.

The success of a rehabilitation program will depend very much on how willing your child is to accept help and guidance. There is no guarantee that it will succeed or that on discharge, your child will not seek out their previous group of friends again and fall back into the same pattern.

Many minors caught up in addiction and sub-cultures that are affiliated with substance abuse will become runaways if there is too much pressure placed on them by their family. It becomes a very fine line; many families cannot live with the dysfunctional, delusional, self-absorbed and manipulative person their child has become. It's very much a double-edged sword. At what point does the family draw the line?

If your child refuses to change it is vital that the rest of the family seek group counseling through professionals who understand addiction and the burden of guilt it places on the family of minor addicts. Ongoing support through groups like Al-Anon and Nar-Anon will also be invaluable to you. These support groups are for the family, friends and loved ones of people in active addiction.

## Parents can Play a Role in Influencing their Child's Choices

The prime role in parenting would be to raise your child to have a positive self-image, realistic view of life and trust you enough to be able to discuss challenging or embarrassing subjects with you. This comes from openly showing love, spending quality time with your child, not speaking at them - but with them, listening to their opinions, asking them how their day went and how they feel, allowing them to make choices and guiding them if their choice is not the best, laughing with your child and always staying interested and in-touch with your child.

This sounds like straightforward parenting, but in the real world of financial pressures, work stresses, marriage problems, divorce and the myriad of daily challenges parents face it is very easy to begin living past your child. Without you realizing, your child could begin to feel lonely and isolated.

A child raised in a trusting and loving environment is less likely to fall in with social sub-cultures or gang-culture. Adolescence, in particular, is a time when a child who feels vulnerable, ignored or inadequate can very easily develop an attachment to a group where they feel accepted. This attachment can become very strong and cause the child to begin evolving into the group-mold and mindset. If you are living past your child, you may not notice the early warning signs and will, therefore, have little chance of excerpting any influence over your child later on.

The evolution from child to adult that we all experience in adolescence is a time of great chemical and hormonal changes in our physiology, and confusion and insecurity as we navigate mental changes. A child in a loving and supportive family environment can generally cope with these changes because they know that they have the necessary emotional support.

The only skill that we are all born with is an innate survival skill. All other skills have to be taught or learned from the people and the environment surrounding us throughout our development. One of the major factors contributing to a predilection to addiction that is not necessarily genetically predisposed is poor coping skills. Even if a person has a predisposition to addiction, but they are raised in a loving supportive environment that equips them with solid coping skills, they may never fall into addiction.

If you as a parent displays poor coping skills that is what you will teach your child! Poor coping skills will exacerbate stress and the inclination to 'medicate' long-term stress through substance abuse or other unhealthy compulsive behavioral patterns has been proven time and again in countless studies conducted worldwide.

Think of a bird being kept in a small cage or on its own without attention. Feather plucking becomes a common behavior pattern. A dog kept on its own without any attention will display unhealthy behavioral patterns like ceaseless barking or falling into depression. The same applies for any animals, birds or reptiles that are, for example, kept in overcrowded conditions; fighting to the death and even cannibalism becomes the norm. All of these behavior patterns are totally alien to the species when they live in their natural environment or are kept as pets that have adequate space on companionship.

Humans are no different! When there is too much stress something has to give, and we begin finding coping mechanisms. These are often substance abuse or other unhealthy and compulsive behavior patterns.

Apart from good parenting and loving attachments to your child, get into the habit of:

- Showing daily interest in your child's activities and sharing your day with your child

- Be open to discussing drug and alcohol abuse, sexual issues, etc with your child; TV programs watched together can often be an initiator (especially true crime programs)

- Tell your child that you love them and encourage them to reciprocate; make hugs a standard

- Share your life with your child by:

    Sharing your childhood and adolescent years

    Admit that you made mistakes and struggled with some issues

    Tell them what you learned from your mistakes and how you resolved issues

    Discuss your hopes and future ambitions

- Share family problems with your child, don't hide them by:

    Admitting to indiscretions in the extended family if there are (like the uncle in jail)

    Explaining that we are not responsible for what happens to other family members

    Avoiding the 'family secret' syndrome that leads to hidden shame

    Openly discussing the circumstances if you are separated from your child's father/mother, explaining the reasons without anger or bitterness

    Not running your previous partner down; your relationship with them is not comparable with the relationship your child may have with them

Reassuring your child that the separation was in no way their fault

Allowing your child to ask questions and answer them honestly

Speaking about death the of a loved one; many people think it caring to shield a child from the reality of death - it's not, it just leaves the child confused

- Allow your child to share their life with you by:

    Encouraging open discussion

    Not overreacting if something they say sounds dicey

    Listening to understand and then discuss the issue

    Not arguing and try to persuade; rather explain and make yourself clear

    Looking to understand your child's feelings and emotions

    Acknowledging that they have been heard and give reassurance

- Appreciate your child and encourage (not demand) reciprocal appreciation by:

    Acknowledging positive changes and behavior

    Guiding your child if they stray or don't understand; be firm, but not harsh

    Saying thank-you and showing appreciation for jobs well done and acts of care or kindness

    Not taking anything for granted

    Praising your child for doing things that deserve praise

- Discuss the world around you and identify life values together by:

  Identifying your own family values

  Asking your child what they view as good and bad values

  Discussing the impact of good and bad values on individuals, family, and society

- Your actions show that you care; lead by example by:

  Setting limits and keeping by your own limits

  Avoiding a 'do as I say and not as I do' mentality; it will be likely met with revolt

  Being consistent in your values, limits, standards and giving love and praise

- Teach your child mutual respect by:

  Not blaming and shaming them (in private or in front of others)

  Not comparing your child negatively to other people; we are all individuals

  Listening to their side and then calmly giving your side; encourage resolution

  Not prying or setting your child up; this is disrespectful and breaks trust

  Teaching your child self-reliance and independence; give them rope with boundaries

  Making your child accept responsibility for their actions or inactions

> Explaining the consequences of not taking responsibility and letting your child experience the consequences in a firm but supportive way

Encourage a healthy lifestyle, not only for your child but for yourself and the rest of the family. Participate in joint activities like outdoor sports, hobbies like art or music, welcome your child's suggestions and make these activities a regular part of your weekly routines.

Of course, despite all your efforts your child can still be exposed to and become involved in a culture of substance abuse and addiction. There is one definite fact though if your child does become an addict, addicts who go into recovery and come from loving and supportive families stand a higher chance of long-term recovery than addicts who do not come from a stable and supportive family background.

# Chapter 6

# Understanding the 3 C's

When you love someone in active addiction or live with them as a parent, spouse or partner it is vital that you educate yourself as much as possible on the subject of substance abuse so that you can fully understand the realities and are able to make the best choices for yourself.

The 3 C's form the core to understanding your role in addiction and deciding whether you can continue living with the addict or whether you must cut them loose.

The 3 C's are:

You did not Cause the addicts predicament; addiction is a choice!

You cannot Cure the addict's disease; choosing recovery from the disease of addiction is a choice!

You cannot Control the addict's disease and its symptoms; recovery is a choice!

The majority of people who love an addict are deeply affected by their loved one's substance abuse and addiction problems. Their emotions are constantly in upheaval. Feelings of helplessness, powerlessness, profound sadness, fear, anger, betrayal and many more negative emotions dominate their everyday. All the while the addict has scant regard for their loved ones.

Unfortunately, addiction is a very powerful disease of the mind and only the addict can opt to seek treatment. An addict in active addiction is no longer the person you once knew. Their brain has been reprogrammed by substances and they cannot control the hold the substances have over them. The disease of addiction renders the addict a self-absorbed, manipulative, deceitful, delusional and often aggressive person who serves only their drug and focuses only on their own need to use. You barely feature in their warped world and you have to accept that.

It is very common for addicts to lay blame on family and loved ones to elicit guilt and deflect attention from themselves. Take responsibility if there is truth in any accusation, but don't take responsibility for the addicts using because of what you may or may not have done! Leave the conversation - you did not cause the addict's substance abuse and addiction problems.

Addicts will manipulate loved ones into trying to get their own way. Stand by what you know and stand your ground. Don't get involved in an argument with the addict because it will be an argument without rules; addicts are master manipulators who will play with words and play with your mind to get what they want. Leave the conversation - you cannot cure their situation!

Addicts will try to coerce you into giving them money, covering for them, lying for them with the promise that if you do this for them they will never ask again, or they will seek treatment, or, or ..... Addicts live in a world of delusion and deception. Stand your ground and leave the conversation. You cannot control the uncontrollable nightmare their life has descended into!

Many people who love an addict fear that if they cut the addict loose the addict will end up living on the streets, turning to crime or prostitution, end up in jail or even end up dead.

Those scenarios are fact! Many addicts end up on the streets living a life of begging or crime. Many of them will end up being processed through the prison system and serve jail time. Ultimately many addicts will end up dead!

As painful as those facts are, you have to accept that it is their choice, not yours. You did not cause their problems, you cannot cure their disease; only they can, and you cannot control their behavior or the outcome and consequences of their actions!

Remember too that if the addict is of legal age, as an adult they are free to live as they please. You cannot and actually have no right to dictate your lifestyle preferences to another adult. By the same token, you do have the right to tell them that their lifestyle is unacceptable to you and unless they are willing to seek professional help and treatment, you no longer want anything further to do with them. You can add that if they are willing to seek professional help and treatment, they will have your absolute support.

Accepting this can be a long process and a bitterly painful experience. So many people repeat over and over again "what happened to my loving son", "where did my beautiful daughter disappear to?", "I don't know this stranger" - and those sad laments are true. The addict is no longer the person you once knew. They have a disease of the mind that has completely transformed them. The person you loved and knew can only come back if the addict is willing to undergo treatment to detoxify their body of all substances, abstain from ever using substances again and undergo extensive psychotherapy to re-program their brain, rewrite their wrongful thought patterns and return them to sanity.

That decision lies wholly and completely in the hands of the addict!

BIELLA BLOM

# Chapter 7

# When to Completely Let Go of an Addict

As terrible as that may sound and as much as you may not want to hear it, there does come a time when in some instances it is best to break all ties with an addict. For many loved ones this can be the most traumatic decision that they will ever have to make, but sometimes it is really a life or death decision.

To remain in active addiction is a choice. To refuse recovery is a choice. If the addict that you love chooses active addiction over recovery, there is nothing at all that you can do!

Many addicts live two lives. One with their addict friends, and the other at home! The problem is that they only return home for money, to steal or to clean up and get a plate of food – usually a combination of all.

The emotional pain and damage that this causes their loved ones are immense, and if there are small children involved it can cause them major psychological damage when they are older. The family tends to wait for the addict to come home and rejoice when they do. The addict does not feel the same way and is often abrasive, detached and even aggressive. The addict may stay for a while, but will inevitably leave again. Behind them sits a heartbroken family who has had their unrealistic expectations dashed once again! They cycle of sitting and waiting in hope that the loving caring person they envisage the addict can become starts again, until the next time their hearts are broken once more.

Because of the effect that substances have on the brain, many addicts become hardened criminals that are not only a danger to the public but to their loved ones as well. Many people who love an addict struggle with this and hold on to the belief that the addict will change. They cling on to the person the addict once was and remain attached to the relationship they shared with the addict before active addiction. There can be a certain point in addiction beyond which recovery becomes very unlikely. The type of drugs being abused also play a major role in an addict's ability to recover if they have been using for a long time.

If an addict threatens your life, don't brush it off. A threat on your life must be taken seriously, even if the addict is your own child. If the addict repeatedly steals from you, report it to the police. If you don't, this will become a life-long pattern! If the addict is arrested, don't pay their bond or bail and if you are called to testify against them - do it! You may still love them, but they stopped loving you the moment they surrendered their life to their substance of choice. Only total sobriety and a strict life-long adherence to a recovery program will re-establish the bond of love and respect that you once shared. Only then can the person you once knew and loved will re-emerge!

In cases where the addict has become abusive, aggressive and a danger to you and your family, you have to let go of the addict; cut them free and tell them that they must never come near you or contact you again. For a parent, this can be soul-destroying, but if you don't do it the consequences for you and the rest of your family could be dire. Also, report the addict's threats and behavior to the local police and apply for a court order preventing the addict from approaching you, any members of your family and coming near your place of work or residence.

If anyone manages to serve this court order on the addict it will probably be met with anger. The addict will very likely try to approach you or enter your home. As soon as you see the addict, call the police and have them arrested!

The addict must know that you are serious this time because they have probably been abusing you and your family for years.

Don't have any guilt feelings over what you have been forced to do. If you are struggling to cope with emotions of guilt and sorrow, seek professional counseling or group counseling if you are a family. Remember, this was not your choice - your hand was forced by the dangerous, aggressive and criminal actions of your loved one, an addict in active addiction! Countless family murders worldwide involved substance abuse. Those parents or partners also probably thought it inconceivable that their child or partner would have it in them to murder their own family. Don't allow yourself and your family to become just another tragic statistic of family murder!

Addicts will very often focus their misplaced anger, self-absorption and self-pity on family members because they know that they can intimidate and manipulate them. They callously and actively prey on the love that they know you have for them. If you cannot give the addict what they want, or start standing your ground against the addict after years of abuse your life could be in very real danger.

Addicts who have fallen into a life of crime most certainly associate with like-minded criminally inclined people. These are not the type of people you want hanging around your home, yourself, your family or your children. These people don't know you, don't care about you and would not hesitate to harm you or steal from you if the opportunity presents itself.

BIELLA BLOM

# Chapter 8

# Medical Treatment for an Addict in Recovery

A major part of guarding recovery is remaining sober and ensuring that no mind-altering substances are ever used at all again! That includes opting for non-alcoholic drinks when there is a toast to the bridal couple at a wedding or any other ceremonial toast, not partaking in sipping alcoholic drinks at religious ceremonies, passing on a helping of the sherry-laced trifle, brandy-laced fruitcake, passing the liqueur chocolate box on without taking one, etc. All seem a bit extreme? No one can gauge the actual state of mind of addict in recovery, sometimes not even the addict. The same goes for the chemical balance of their brain; no one knows. Total abstinence is a definite guarantee for sobriety. Total abstinence is a definite guarantee that there will be no backslide.

The same rule applies to any habit-forming drug. Total abstinence is the only way!

Unfortunately, addicts in recovery, like other people do become ill, get injured, require surgery or fall pregnant. This means that the doctors will have to use strong drugs to control pain, clear infections, maintain sedation, etc. For an addict in recovery, this means walking on a knife-edge!

Part of the recovery program instills a life of honesty, vigilance, faith, and trust in a higher power or God. An addict who has succeed in staying clean and sober and maintaining their recovery has accepted these three lifestyle choices and they have become second nature.

At times of illness, trauma or surgery it is to these three steps that the addict and their loved ones must turn.

If it is known beforehand that the recovering-addict is going to require surgery or medication for any reason, they must be open and honest with the doctor about their past substance abuse and that they are in recovery. For many addicts, the idea of such a disclosure fills them with fear because of the social stigma attached to addiction. Very few medical doctors or other medical practitioners will judge badly. Most are well versed in the problem of substance abuse and the challenges faced by recovering addicts. To know that the addict is now in recovery and willing to guard their recovery by honest disclosure will most likely earn respect and careful consideration in the choice of drugs used in treatment.

In the event of an unexpected medical emergency, prior agreements must be made with the recovering addict's parents, partner, spouse, family, and friends that they will inform doctors and medical practitioners (even first responders) that the patient is a recovering-addict and that they have a prior history of substance abuse. There is no place here for shame or pride! Medical treatment could inadvertently place hard-earned recovery on the line. No addict in recovery is ever more than a hair's breadth away from relapse.

If the patient is an alcoholic in recovery, the same applies. Many medicines contain very high levels of alcohol.

Depending on the medical condition, it may be inevitable that powerful drugs form part of the treatment to facilitate healing. If potentially habit-forming drugs are refused, depending on the medical condition the recovering-addict could die, so reason must prevail. Also, the body must recover medically as quickly as possible to limit exposure to drug treatment.

During the recovery stage from the illness, injury or surgery but while still on treatment openly ask the doctor and nursing staff about medication being administered. The recovering-addict must be honest about actual pain levels, and if they no longer need pain control drugs, this must be relayed to the doctor. Loving family encouragement and support in situations like these is vital.

The recovering-addict must be very vigilant of how they are reacting to the effect the medication is having on them. Have they started looking forward to the next dose? If so, it's time for prayer and meditation. Get back into what the recovery program has taught them. They must be honest with themselves, loved ones and the medical team. Loved ones must encourage open and honest communication without stress and nagging. Show your support and show that you believe in the addict's recovery!

If the recovering-addict admits that any medication is starting to have a hold on them, tell the doctor and ask if there are alternatives that may not have the same mind-altering effect. Keep encouraging honesty - the addict's recovery is on the line!

When the recovering-addict gets a renewed prescription, lovingly discuss their physical symptoms and ask if a renewed prescription is necessary. Remind them to analyze their physical symptoms and then analyze their thought patterns. Are they telling them-self that they still need certain drugs when in fact they don't? Addiction is a disease of deception, and that includes self-deception. Encourage the recovering-addict to come clean, confess their truth through prayer and meditation, and get them-self back into a recovery program as soon as possible if they think they may be backsliding. In-patient, out-patient, whatever but get back them into a recovery program without delay. Go with them to the rooms, support their honesty that they are at risk of backsliding and relapse. They will find the support they need, and if your loved one has been in recovery for some time you will be surprised at how willing they are to maintain their recovery.

Keep reaching out for support together and keep being honest. Attend group therapy sessions, together re-read the books that they were given in the early stages of recovery, do whatever it takes to guard the addict's recovery.

Life happens to everyone, and life happens to addicts in recovery. They have been equipped with the tools to cope with life on life's terms and have admitted that they cannot maintain their recovery without the support and guidance of a higher power, of a loving God. They know what to do; do it with them and guard their recovery!

# Chapter 9

# Coping with the Death of an Addict

Any death is a profoundly painful experience for the loved ones of the deceased. The death of a child also comes with the false belief that 'parents should not bury their children; children bury their parents.' This statement is, of course, a false-truth that is repeated over and over in society leading to additional unnecessary pain and guilt. Babies, children, and young adults have died since time began and were buried by their parents. Don't let this false-truth add to your pain and grief!

An addict lifestyle exposes addicts to life-threatening situations every day. The substance abuse in itself threatens the addicts' life through accidental overdose, poor quality drugs laced with anything from talcum powder to rat poison and physiological conditions like heart, liver, and kidney failure. Addicts who inject can die from sepsis contracted from dirty needles or contract Hepatitis B which is a potentially life-threatening liver infection caused by the hepatitis B virus (HBV), also from sharing needles.

In addition, many addicts turn to crime like opportunistic theft, burglaries, and armed robberies or dealing (selling drugs). They are placing their lives and the lives of innocent people on the line daily. It is common for female addicts to turn to prostitution; some adolescent boys and adult males will do the same. Prostitution is a very dangerous profession if practiced from street corners and many prostitutes are often abused and beaten by their clients.

These assaults are never reported to the police by the prostitute and that means that crimes committed against prostitutes are an accepted part of the trade. Murder of prostitutes is also very common and often not investigated because of societies' scorn and disrespect of prostitutes and addicts.

Because addicts are intoxicated and their inhibitions are lowered, and in many cases, their sense of physical strength is heightened, addicts regularly get involved in brawls and it is not uncommon for dangerous weapons like firearms, knives and broken bottles to be introduced the fracas. Many intoxicated addicts commit murder and deeply regret their actions once they are sober. Their addiction problem is not an excuse, but it would be the reason that they committed murder.

Addicts also die from less dramatic incidents like motor vehicle accidents if driving under the influence, being run over by a vehicle as they stumble along aimlessly right into the face of on-coming traffic. They can drown in a bath of water if they pass-out and their head becomes submerged. Fire is another hazard in the addicts' life because addicts pass-out with a lit cigarette in their hand, and that eventually sets fire to the mattress or chair that they are on. By the time that the addict regains consciousness (if they do at all) they can have complications from smoke inhalation (which can be fatal) or severe burns and die from infection because their bodies are too compromised to fight off infection. Another fire hazard is candles. Addicts often use a candle to heat and dissolve substances that they are going to inject themselves with. If they pass-out without putting the candle out first and the lit candle falls over it will cause a fire in the area directly around the now unconscious addict.

It is also very common for an addict to commit suicide. Sometimes addicts take an unintentional overdose but mostly the overdose is intentional. Addicts also hang them-self, slit their wrists and shoot them-self to commit suicide. Many addicts who have hit rock-bottom desperately want to come clean, but they either don't believe that they can leave their drug and seek help, or they don't know who to turn to. The reality is that help and understanding are always at hand and the death of these addicts is tragic and unnecessary. That is why it is vital that as much media and public exposure is given to the problem of substance abuse, and the message that there is a solution is a reality!

Society holds a common perception that suicide is a cowardly act. Nothing could be further from the truth! The only skill we are born with is the instinctive skill to survive. There are countless reports of children and adults surmounting impossible odds by doing things way beyond their normal capabilities to survive in life-threatening situations.

Suicide then goes completely against the only instinctive skill we have! To fly in the face of the instinctive skill to survive does not take courage; it takes the direst form of desperation! A desperation that completely overwhelms our survival instinct and equips us with the courage to take our own life! Suicide is when the problems we are faced with appear to us to be so extreme and dire that we can see no way out. We conclude that death is the only way we can escape this burden and desperation gives us the courage to take our own life.

Substance abuse and addiction put the users' life in danger every day, and addicts in active addiction will confirm that they know this but they can't or don't want to stop using.

## Processing the Premature Death of your Loved One

Educating yourself on the realities of loving an addict right from when you first confirm that they are in active addiction will open your eyes to the reality of their problem, the dangers of the lifestyle that they have chosen and prepare you for the fact that they dance with death every day that they are in active addiction.

You have to accept that there was nothing that you could have done to prevent the death, and there is nothing that you did that caused the death. Guilt is the ever-present wretched companion of people who love an addict who died. Guilt is a pointless and wasted emotion that will negatively impact your life if you do not find a means to rid yourself of it and come to terms with the reality that you were powerless over the situation that played itself out at the time of your loved one's death.

Even if you let go of the addict; chased them from your home and obtained a restraining order, you did that out of self-preservation and also for the sake of other family members. It was not a choice it was a necessity because of the addict's delinquent and dangerous behavior. Had you not have done that your life would have stayed a living hell, and that addict would probably have died at the same time by the same means because they chose to continue living their addicted delinquent lifestyle.

## Rid yourself of Guilt and Blame

Once the initial shock abates and you are left with the profound sorrow and grief, as with any death you must seek additional emotional support to help you through the process. Grieving the death of an addict comes with the additional pain of guilt, self-blame, questioning yourself, your right to have been a parent a partner or spouse. Although normal, you must have professional support to process these thoughts and emotions and then detach yourself from them. You do not deserve to suffer for the rest of your life because your loved someone who chose addiction and rejected recovery. It is not your burden to bear!

Find a grief counselor, a therapist who deals with addiction or attend Nar-Anon or Al-Anon group therapy sessions for support from people who can identify with your pain. Also, seek spiritual support through whichever religion or spiritual belief you hold. It is vital that you get support from people who understand addiction and know that whatever your loved one did or became, you will always love them and you have every right to.

Broader society can be very judgemental and the death of an addict is often met with cold callousness. Don't let that attitude touch you; you loved the addict and genuine love never dies. Also, don't carry any shame that society may place upon you. You need never be ashamed of the addict that you love and you need never be ashamed that you love and addict who has died in active addiction. Lying to society to keep face means lying to yourself, and lying to your-self will invite depression and other emotional ills into your life. You owe society nothing, and anyone who judges you or your departed loved one is not worth knowing!

Print and keep Three 3 C's somewhere where you can readily read and re-read them:

- You did not Cause the addicts predicament; addiction is a choice!

- You could not Cure the addict's disease; choosing recovery from the disease of addiction is a choice!

- You could not Control the addict's disease and its symptoms; recovery is a choice!

BIELLA BLOM

# Chapter 10

# Commonly Abused Substances

The market is flooded with many mind-altering substances, some illegal and others legal (alcohol, prescription and over-the-counter). It would be impossible to cover all the substances in this book. Listed are the more commonly used substances, many of which will form the base-substances of combinations sold on the streets, in pharmacies or prescribed by doctors under different names.

## Alcohol

Alcohol is the most commonly abused substance worldwide and has, and continues to destroy the lives of countless people and families, often creating a cycle of substance abuse and dysfunction that is passed from one generation to the next.

### The Effects of Alcohol Abuse

In low doses, alcohol depresses the inhibitory activity of the brain. The removal of inhibition leads to unopposed excitatory brain activity and elicits stimulatory behavior.

At higher doses, alcohol depresses the excitatory activity of the brain, leading to sedation.

The effects of progressively increasing doses of alcohol include slight muscular incoordination, slight sensory impairment, talkativeness, sociability, and euphoria, marked mental impairment, clumsiness, unsteadiness, prolonged reaction time, intoxicated behaviour, emotional lability, nausea, vomiting, double vision, marked ataxia (full loss of control of bodily movements), hypothermia, marked speech impairment, signs of general anaesthesia, coma, respiratory failure and eventually death.

Alcoholism is alcohol dependence, in short addiction! Alcoholism is one of the most overlooked, untreated, treatable diseases in the world!

### *Physical and Mental Complications of Alcohol Abuse*

The most common causes of death following chronic alcohol abuse are cirrhosis of the liver, cancers of the respiratory, gastrointestinal tract, heart disease, and suicide. Other complications include:

- Malnutrition

- Erosion of the gastrointestinal tract causing ulceration, bleeding and mal-absorption of vitamins, minerals and vital nutrients

- Impaired liver function

- Irreversible damage to peripheral nerve tissue leading to pain, pins, and needles, poor circulation and tissue death in the extremities that can lead to gangrene and amputations

- Damage to the brain that can lead to potentially irreversible ataxia, memory loss, psychotic behavior and dementia

- Hypertension, atherosclerosis and heart damage

- Anaemia, poor immune reactions, and impaired blood clotting
- Hormonal abnormalities
- Sexual and reproductive impairment
- Muscle tissue damage and degeneration

### *Alcohol Withdrawal Symptoms*

Severe alcohol withdrawal especially delirium tremens (rapid onset of confusion) is potentially life-threatening and must be treated as a medical emergency. Alcohol withdrawal for addicts who want to come clean and dry must be managed under professional medical supervision and not attempted by the addict at home.

Symptoms of alcohol withdrawal include:

- Nausea and vomiting
- Tremors (the shakes)
- Sweating and flushes
- Severe headache
- Restlessness and agitation
- Increased pulse rate
- Rise in blood pressure
- Fever
- Electrolyte disturbances and dehydration
- Hallucinations

- Seizures

The complications and withdrawal symptoms bring home the fact that alcohol is a drug. A dangerous drug! Despite the social acceptance of alcohol use and the constant denial that it is not a drug.

# Marijuana (Cannabis)

Despite the rise in social acceptance of marijuana and pressure on governments to legalize the use, marijuana is a dangerous habit-forming drug. The claims that it has medicinal qualities are founded, and most drugs have medicinal qualities if used sparingly and only to treat specific medical conditions. Overuse leads to addiction and addiction leads to mental and physiological complications.

Marijuana, like alcohol, is considered by many medical professionals (and addicts in recovery) to be a gateway drug. Using marijuana lowers the users' inhibitions, leaving them open to suggestion and more inclined to try other drugs. This leads to further addiction to more hard-core substances or prescription drugs.

### *The Effects of Marijuana Abuse*

Marijuana is derived from the fibrous hemp plant (Cannabis Sativa). The leaves, flower-tops, stems, and seeds of the plant are harvested, broken down and sold as marijuana. The concentrated resin of the plant is also harvested and commonly sold as hashish. Marijuana is known by many different names in countries and cities around the world. Marijuana is often mixed with other drugs to give the user a better high.

Marijuana is most commonly smoked in hand-rolled cigarettes or in pipes, but it can be chewed, eaten as an ingredient in food or steeped and made into a tea.

People abuse marijuana for the mind-altering or hallucinogenic effects and also the euphoric and sedative properties. Marijuana brings on feelings of elation, reduced anxiety, a feeling of wellbeing, increased sociability, enhancement of pleasant sensations and sensory perceptions.

Marijuana has a strong psychological dependence producing effect. Many users argue that it does not have a physiological dependence effect, but as users experience physiological withdrawal symptoms when they stop using, that belief is a myth.

## *Physical and Mental Complications of Marijuana Abuse*

Continued (daily) abuse of marijuana leads to a combination of complications, including:

- Distortion of time perception; minutes seem like hours or vice-versa

- Distortion of distance perception that leads to impaired skills when driving, using tools or machinery and puts the user in danger if they are walking in public (misjudging cars when crossing a road, stairs, escalators, etc.)

- Short-term memory impairment, negatively affecting work or educational performance

- Very short concentration span, negatively affecting work or educational performance and also endangering household safety (putting on a stove, opening a tap, leaving a cigarette or candle burning, etc and then forgetting about it)

- Irritability, anxiety and psychotic episodes

- Respiratory congestion

- Constant coughing, bronchitis and even emphysema or lung cancer

- Inflamed whites of the eyes
- Increased appetite and sugar cravings
- Hypoglycaemia
- Loss of appetite if severely abused
- Dry mouth and thirst - dehydration
- Ever- increasing feeling of apathy and energy loss
- Withdrawal into a fantasy world and withdrawal from relationships and society as a whole
- Losing interest in a functional lifestyle, work, education, home and turning to dysfunction, crime and often a 'street life'
- Hormonal disturbances and potential infertility

**Marijuana Withdrawal Symptoms**

- Sleep disturbances
- Irritability
- Restlessness
- Decreased appetite
- Sweating

Long-term abuse of marijuana not only leads to the abuse of harder drugs but also decent into a dysfunctional lifestyle and often crime.

# Cocaine

Cocaine and crack cocaine are highly addictive and dangerous drugs that are responsible for dereliction of users worldwide. Most cocaine users are unable to remain functional for long after they start regular use.

**The Effects of Cocaine Abuse**

Cocaine is derived from the leaves the coca plant (Erythroxylum Coca) that originates from South America. Cocaine is known by many different names in countries and cities around the world.

Street cocaine consists of cocaine salt (directly derived from the plant leaves) and diluted or cut with a combination of other chemical substances at a ratio of one part cocaine salt to ten parts of the other components. The dilution of components depends very much on the integrity of the dealer. It can range from lethal toxins to harmless talcum powder. Street cocaine is sold in a white powder form

Street cocaine is most commonly snorted, but can also be swallowed or rubbed into the gums.

Crack cocaine is street cocaine treated to chemically extract the purified cocaine alkaloid. This process leaves the cocaine in crystal form (hence 'crack' cocaine).

Crack cocaine is cheaper and generally smoked. It is often mixed with tobacco or marijuana for smoking.

Both forms of cocaine lead to a state of stimulation and euphoria, a feeling of great power, energy, mental ability, talkativeness, sociability and sexual stimulation. Cocaine is highly addictive. The high is often short-lived, particularly with crack cocaine, leading the user to crave more and more. As tolerance grows daily usage gradually increases to achieve the same high.

The rebound after a high includes depression and lethargy. These extremes in the experience of the high and coming down is what leads the user to cravings and chasing their next high. Binging on cocaine is very common. While on a binge the user will not eat or sleep and a binge can continue for up to two days, or until the user's body collapses into a very deep sleep. On waking they will be very depressed, lethargic and often hungry and dehydrated. The cycle then starts all over again!

***Physical and Mental Complications of Cocaine Abuse***

Continued abuse of cocaine will lead to growing severity of the physical and mental complications suffered by the user. Complications include:

- Dilated pupils
- Cardiac stimulation and hypertension
- Pale complexion
- Rapid shallow respiration
- Hyperthermia
- Paranoid psychosis
- Delusions of persecution, often resulting in violent behavior
- Malnutrition and emaciation
- Nasal damage, constant sniffing, nose bleeds and often permanent damage to, or collapse of the nasal septum (sniffing street cocaine)
- Loss of the senses of smell and taste (sniffing street cocaine)
- Lung damage and edema (smoking crack cocaine)

- Hypertension leading to brain hemorrhages
- Visual disturbances
- Bowel problems
- Sexual dysfunction
- Constant itchy skin leading to scratching and scabbing

Cocaine overdose is a very serious condition and immediate medical treatment is vital. Cocaine overdoses will be fatal without urgent medical intervention. Overdose characteristics and causes of death include:

- Seizures
- Hyperthermia
- Cardiac arrest
- Respiratory arrest

*Cocaine Withdrawal Symptoms*

A cocaine addict who wants to attempt to come clean and stop using must never try going through withdrawal on their own at home. The withdrawal must be managed under strict medical supervision.

- Severe muscle aches
- Spasms
- Nausea, vomiting, and diarrhea
- Severe stomach cramps
- Elevated heartbeat and palpitations

- Hypotension

- Agitation and restlessness

- Severe depression

- Thoughts of suicide (very real)

Cocaine abuse leads to uncontrollable compulsive behavior, leaving the addict unable to focus on normal daily responsibilities. Invariably long-term abusers of cocaine will turn to lives of crime and prostitution because they are unable to keep a job and do not comply with acceptable social norms and rules, so their home lives disintegrate.

# Heroin

Heroin is a chemically modified form of morphine. Heroin is a derivative of opium which is the dried extract from green poppy (Papaver Somniferum). It is sold in the form of brown cakes or lumps.

Street heroin is invariably diluted with a plethora of substances, being anything from toxins to harmless 'fillers' to bulk-up the weight as it is sold per gram.

### The Effects of Heroin Abuse

Heroin produces a pleasant dream-like state that alleviates stress, fatigue, depression, and anxiety. Heroin can also lead to a state of outright euphoria. Heroin is either smoked o injected. Heroin can very quickly lead to abuse and daily use as it is a highly addictive drug. It leads to physiological and psychological dependence.

### *Physical and Mental Complications of Heroin Abuse*

Complication of heroin use will become more serious as the addict begins to use more regularly and the longer the addiction continues. Complications include:

- Constricted pupils

- Sedation to the point of unconsciousness

- Nausea (although the addict can eventually develop a tolerance, making nausea cease)

- Respiratory center depression

- Infections and contracting transferable diseases related to constant self-injecting ( sharing needles and unhygienic environments)

- Malnutrition and emaciation

- Compromised immune system

- Constipation and bowel disease

Heroin overdose is a very serious condition and immediate medical treatment is vital. Heroin overdoses will be fatal without urgent medical intervention. Overdose characteristics and causes of death include:

- Respiratory depression

- Brain damage from prolonged respiratory depression leaving the brain starved of oxygen

- Reduced body temperature with cold and clammy skin

- Pulmonary oedema

- Cardiovascular collapse
- Coma

**Heroin Withdrawal Symptoms**

As with other drugs, a heroin addict who wants to attempt to come clean and stop using must never try going through withdrawal on their own at home. The withdrawal must be managed under strict medical supervision.

- Severe body pains and aches
- Hot and cold sweats
- Agitation and restlessness
- Flu-like symptoms
- Nausea, vomiting, and diarrhea
- Hallucinations
- Severe depression
- Paranoia or psychosis

Heroin abuse is a very difficult addiction to break and heroin addicts need constant psychotherapy and medical care while in recovery. Heroin addiction also leads to uncontrollable compulsive behavior, leaving the addict unable to focus on normal daily responsibilities. Invariably long-term abusers of heroin will turn to lives of crime and prostitution because they are unable to keep a job and do not comply with acceptable social norms and rules, so their home lives disintegrate. They also often have very serious health problems that are left untreated leaving them frail and vulnerable.

# Conclusion

Addiction is a disease, and many people are genetically predisposed to the disease of addiction. Not everyone who is predisposed will become an addict.

Social conditions, the home environment, and an individual's coping skills are the ultimate catalysts that will dictate whether an individual will fall into active addiction. Addiction can be compulsive behavioral patterns, or the compulsive use of mind-altering substances. A combination of compulsive behavioral patterns together with the compulsive use of mind-altering drugs is very common among addicts.

Drug addicts are not 'bad people' who should be shamed and rejected by society. There are many drug addicts who are highly intelligent people, kind and caring, loving and open-hearted, who would make this world a better place, make wonderful parents, siblings, children - their potential is endless, if only they could stay clean and sober.

Never feel ashamed of loving an addict; never feel guilty about the addict's lifestyle!

Loving an addict in active addiction is living through the hell of their disease, and living through the hell of your powerlessness over the situation.

Addicts in active addiction can not only make your life a living hell, but they can be a threat to your safety and wellbeing. Let go and detach yourself from the addict when you can no longer live with them. Detach yourself without guilt; let go of them with love and empathy. Know that there is nothing at all that you can do to change the situation.

Be kind to yourself, forgive yourself, rebuild your self-respect, learn to love yourself again. Yes, you made mistakes - no one is perfect, but the addict in active addiction is choosing their lifestyle. If the addict that you love finds sobriety, goes into a rehabilitation center follows through on a lifelong recovery program and reaches out to you again, you could very well rediscover the beautiful person that you once knew and still love. There is always hope!

It is believed by many that addicts who are in recovery and very dedicated to their recovery are some of the best people to love. This is because:

- They are honest
- They are humble
- They have empathy and forgive
- They do not judge
- They will give a second chance
- They accept life on life's terms
- They know the value of life
- They appreciate the importance of family and genuine friends
- They are dedicated and disciplined
- They have very strong spiritual values, like faith and love
- They understand that everyone is different
- The accommodate these differences

Why? Because an addict who is dedicated to their recovery is doing so to keep living the miracle of recovery! They know what it is like to dance with death, to lose everything they valued, to lose them-self, to become enslaved to an unstoppable compulsion that destroyed their lives, to watch their bodies slowly die, to live the life of the walking dead, to live on the dark side of life!

# Where to Find More Information and Support

Most people have no idea what to do when faced with a loved one who is caught up in active addiction. Very few people are educated in the dynamics behind substance abuse and people keep asking "why can't you just stop?"

Addicts can't 'just stop'! They are caught up in the disease of addiction and they need medical and professional help to get them onto the path of recovery. Unfortunately choosing recovery is the addict's choice, not yours.

For the loved ones of an addict in active addiction finding valuable information can be like trying to find a needle in a haystack! You need to be educated about the challenges that you are facing. There are many publications and websites on the challenges and facts of substance abuse, but for the uninitiated, the first stop should be Narcotics Anonymous, Alcoholics Anonymous, Al-Anon and Nar-Anon depending on whether your loved one is addicted to alcohol or to drugs.

Alcoholics Anonymous offers support to alcoholics in recovery, but you will find valuable information on their site to help you understand your loved one's disease and problems. You can buy books in print and online that will educate you. The world site will also guide you to support groups in your country and city.

https://www.aa.org/

Narcotics Anonymous offers support to drug addicts in recovery, but you will find valuable information on their site to help you understand your loved one's disease and problems. You can buy books in print and online that will educate you. The world site will also guide you to support groups in your country and city.

https://www.na.org/

Al-Anon offers support to the family and loved ones of alcoholics in active addiction as well as alcoholics who died as a result of their disease. This is where you will find support, reassurance, and comfort for yourself, be able to discuss your pain and fears with people who share those same emotions. The world site will also guide you to support groups in your country and city.

https://al-anon.org/

Nar-Anon offers support to the family and loved ones of drug addicts in active addiction as well as drug addicts who died as a result of their disease. This is where you will find support, reassurance, and comfort for yourself, be able to discuss your pain and fears with people who share those same emotions. The world site will also guide you to support groups in your country and city.

http://www.nar-anon.org/

*Every saint has a past and every sinner has a future*

– Oscar Wilde

LIVING WITH AN ADDICT

Behind the successful front, survivor of drug addiction, alcoholism, self-destructive behavior, toxic relationships, domestic violence, depression and more as I tried desperately to find society's acceptance and approval.

Through total surrender – a point where I genuinely begged the God I had always refused to recognize for help; a dim light of hope appeared. Unable to carry on living as I was any longer I actively sought help and found it. I began to find healing.

Once you find self-love and self-acceptance, no judgment or retribution can touch you; you find the freedom to be yourself. Once you accept the presence of an ever-present, ever-loving spiritual power that is much greater than you, you can relax, stop trying to control everything and finally live. The dim light of hope becomes ever brighter until it completely embraces you and eventually begins to radiate from you. Let go and let God!

- **Biella Blom**

BIELLA BLOM

*Win a free*

# kindle
# OASIS

Let us know what you thought of this book to enter the sweepstake at:

http://booksfor.review/livingwithaddict